What ar

Written by Maoliosa Kelly
Illustrated by Beccy Blake
Photographed by Antony Elworthy

Collins

3

8

Wooo Wooo Wooo Wooo!

13

What am I?

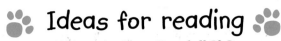 Ideas for reading

Written by Clare Dowdall PhD
Lecturer and Primary Literacy Consultant

Learning objectives: use language to imagine and recreate roles and experiences; read a range of familiar and common words and simple sentences independently; show an understanding of how information can be found in non-fiction books to answer questions about where, who, why and how

Curriculum links: Communication, Language and Literacy: Use language to imagine and recreate roles and experiences; Knowledge and Understanding of the World:

Find out about events in the lives of people they know; Creative Development: Use imagination in role play; express and communicate ideas by using role play

Interest words: what, am, I

Resources: Some props that identify different types of job e.g. a whistle for a teacher, a hard hat for a builder

Getting started

- Ask the children what they would like to do when they grow up and create a list of different jobs. Help children to take turns and listen to each other.
- Look at the front cover and discuss what jobs the children in the photo might do.
- Practise reading the title. Use a finger to trace the words from left to right.
- Dwell on the word *what* and the question mark. Discuss what the question mark does. Ask the children to think of questions to ask the characters on the front cover.
- Read the questions on the back cover together.

Reading and responding

- Look at p1 together. Ask the children to describe what is happening in the picture and who the characters are (*vet, owner, pet*).
- Practise reading the question *What am I?* together again.
- Turn to pp 2–3. Ask pairs to talk about who the person is and what job she does (*doctor*).